BORO

A Concise Informative Guide
To Everything You Need To
Know About Boro; Important
Information Everyone Needs

Audrey Griffith

Table of Contents

CHAPTER ONE

Boro

Boro is a traditional patchwork technique that developed more for practical reasons than for their inherent beauty. Boro, literally "ragged" or "tattered," was a popular look amongst rural Japanese in the late nineteenth and early twentieth centuries. Because cotton did not become widely available in Japan until the early twentieth century, it was normal practice for women to use sashiko stitching to repair holes in kimonos and futon covers as they became worn.

'Boro' first appeared in rural Japan between the years 1850 and 1950. Humble peasant farmers of the time invented the method to keep warm during times of great cold and destitution.

Boro clothing exemplifies the Japanese principle of "mottainai," which means "not wasting fabric" (here, cloth) when one may extend the cloth's usable life by recycling and reuse. The patchwork construction and repaired appearance of these handcrafted garments were telltale signs. These garments typically had several sashiko stitches to secure the many layers of cloth, which were often of wildly contrasting colors and patterns.

These fabrics would be passed down through families and given several patches over the years, to the point where an outsider may not be able to tell where the original cloth ended and the patches started. What we now find attractive is something that was formerly considered unseemly in Japan because it was covered in indigo fragments. Some postwar Japanese found boro textiles depressing since they were a reminder of their country's poverty.

The boro style gradually lost favor as Japan entered the modern age and mass-produced goods became the norm in the industrial economy. Now, people appreciate them for what they truly are: tangible remnants of Japan's past. For fans of raw denim, it's important to note that boro was as practical as a pair of denim overalls from the eighteenth century.

HISTORY

Between 1850 and 1950, 'boro' was developed in rural Japan. Humble peasant farmers of the time invented the method to keep warm during times of great cold and destitution.

The Sashiko process is used to sew and mend layers upon layers of patchworked cotton (or hemp) textiles over the course of many years. It was a time of great thrift because of the high demand for Cotton; nothing was thrown away. This outfit was made to symbolize the hard work and perseverance of poor agricultural families throughout the years.

Boro means "tattered" or "repaired" in Japanese, which is where the word "boroboro" comes from.

After World War II, Japan's culture began modernizing, and its practitioners of this folk art joyfully abandoned it. Boro clothing is a humiliating symbol of the working class in Japan's past.

Young designers and collectors today place a high value on vintage indigo cottons and Boro clothing because of the historical significance and aesthetic appeal they find in the style's original impact

Made in the USA, by Farm Wives and Fishermen's Wives, 1850-1900

Boro textiles reflect the story of a resilient people who overcame extreme hardship by employing a wide variety of ingenious and resourceful techniques. In order to keep their husbands warm during the bitter winters, these resourceful wives would sew extra layers onto their husbands' work clothes. As a means of increasing insulation and prolonging the life of their garments, they patched worn spots using remnants of fabric and stitched them together using sashiko.

Poor Japanese farm wives had to spend their days until the

early 20th century spinning cotton fibers into threads or yarn and then weaving them on hand looms into fabric for their families' apparel and household goods. Jackets, vests, and momohiki and monpe trousers were the most prevalent "noragi" outfits. "Noragi" is the Japanese word for handcrafted, hand-stitched country labor apparel. Every Japanese farmer's or fisherman's wife was expected to know how to sew, and this skill was passed down from mother to daughter down the generations.

The Japanese countryside favored the indigo blue dye "aizome" for its textiles for a variety of reasons. Aside from its monetary and cultural significance, indigo was revered by the Japanese because of the widespread belief that it reflected the color of the waters around the Japanese islands. Indigo plants were common and flourished wild all over the Japanese islands. Indigo dye was chosen because it allowed blue fabrics to retain their color even after years of wear and tear. Nonetheless, with repeated washes and usage, the blue-dyed linen faded into a lovely lighter blue or blues.

Indigo is naturally antimicrobial and has the added benefit of being able to withstand smells. Clothing dyed with indigo was also believed to have curative medical effects for a variety of skin issues. The belief among farmers that indigo dye naturally repelled insects and snakes is an interesting cultural quirk. This idea is the fundamental explanation for why indigo attire was so popular among Japanese farm women. (Japanese women worked in the fields alongside their husbands).

These aforementioned housewives constantly had to minimize, reuse, and recycle the family's textiles for economical and practical reasons because they lived in isolated, destitute rural areas.

They painstakingly dissembled old futon covers, worn out clothes, and other ragged home materials to recycle and refashion the useable bits into tough field-work "noragi" gear. Disassembled textiles were sometimes re-dyed to give them a new lease of life. The faint impression of a tsutsugaki or katazome pattern on the back of a boro jacket is only one example of how a textile's history may sometimes be deduced via careful examination.

Nowadays, many who admire the modest practices of a rural Japanese woman's textile saving, reuse, and repurposing... wear and textiles from Japan, boro, people are able to feel and touch such priceless relics of a bygone era for themselves.

It's fitting that today's most prestigious contemporary Japanese businesses are ushering boro into the 21st century. One such label is Kapital, which has introduced boro denim outerwear, denim, and a tote bag. The outfits and materials are deconstructed in the style of traditional boro clothing. In the past, people did this because they had to, but now, we do it because we value our heritage.

An other Japanese company carrying the boro torch is Koromo. A long-sleeved denim shirt featuring boro patches at the back of the neck is an illustration of one of their products.

CHAPTER TWO

CONNECTION BY MEANS OF BORO STITCHING

Recent fashions in repairing and patching clothing have been inspired by the traditional Japanese arts of boro and sashiko. Some people use these names interchangeably, although there are really two separate groups.

Boro is a Japanese name that literally means "tattered or mended" since it is derived from the term boroboro. This method of mending and patching utilizes many layers of fabric and a running thread to create a seamless repair. These textiles were produced by reusing scraps of clothing and other materials that had been properly stored, including handspun and indigo-dyed textiles.

Due to the labor-intensive nature of producing the raw materials and finished fabric (typically hemp), this method of repairing arose out of necessity. Since cotton wasn't widely available in Japan until the 20th century, boro stitching was used to painstakingly repair worn out kimonos and futon covers. Carefully fixed by makers, these fabrics were passed down and repaired numerous times.

The roots of boro are lost to time, however it is believed that the art form originated as a home craft in Japan during the Edo period (1615-1868). Boro fabric was born out of need and was worn and used by destitute rural communities, therefore very little of the early work survives. As a symbol of their previous poverty, boro mended clothes was stigmatized for a long time. Modern art enthusiasts frequently prefer the back of a boro cloth because of its impromptu and abstract design.

What a relief it is to see this method of fixing things making a comeback. It's a hobby anyone can try, and it goes against the current fast fashion trend of mass-market retailers producing cheap clothing quickly (often poorly made, using cheap fabrics and impoverished labor) in response to the newest trends, which are meant to be consumed and discarded as soon as they go out of style.

The process of mending our beloved garments, I've discovered, has more significance than just fixing the fabric. In addition to improving our physical health, taking this time and space may help restore our mental health as well. Fixing anything allows you to slow down and appreciate the physical object you're working on. Because we care enough to devote our time, we love and cherish the clothes we've made.

Now that you know what boro is and how it got started, you can easily recognize it when you see it, both in its pure form and in the form that has been inspired by boro, in products from some of your favorite companies.

THE END